101 QUIZZES for BFFs

CRAZY FUN TESTS TO SEE WHO KNOWS WHO BEST!

Natasha Burton

adamsmedia
AVON, MASSACHUSETTS

For Jenn, Ciji, and Alana, my best friends (forever and ever).

Published by
Adams Media, a division of F+W Media, Inc.
57 Littlefield Street, Avon, MA 02322. U.S.A.
www.adamsmedia.com

ISBN 10: 1-4405-8420-6
ISBN 13: 978-1-4405-8420-6
eISBN 10: 1-4405-8421-4
eISBN 13: 978-1-4405-8421-3

Printed by RR Donnelley, Harrisonburg, VA, U.S.A.
10 9 8 7 6 5 4 3 2 1
October 2014

Library of Congress Cataloging-in-Publication Data

Burton, Natasha.
  101 quizzes for BFFs / Natasha Burton.
    pages cm
  ISBN 978-1-4405-8420-6 (pb) -- ISBN 1-4405-8420-6 (pb) -- ISBN 978-1-4405-8421-3 (ebook) -- ISBN 1-4405-8421-4 (ebook)
  1. Friendship--Miscellanea. I. Title. II. Title: One hundred one quizzes for BFFs.
BJ1533.F8B874 2014
177'.62--dc23

                                          2014029037

Cover design by Frank Rivera.
Cover image © blue67/123RF.

This book is available at quantity discounts for bulk purchases.
For information, please call 1-800-289-0963.

Acknowledgments

Thank you to the team at Adams Media, especially Brendan O'Neill and Christine Dore for entrusting me with this project, and my editor Meredith O'Hayre. I am also so appreciative of everyone at Jean V. Naggar Literary Agency for guiding me through my career, especially my wonderful, patient, and oh-so-talented agent Elizabeth Evans. Thank you for making my "become a published author" dreams come true.

Because this is a book about friendship, I bow down to my three best friends, Jennifer Jacobson, Alana Newell, and Ciji Saso, for being there for me always (well, since I was nine, four, and seven, respectively). I love you guys and don't know what I would do without you three in my life. (Special shout-out to Alana for keeping us all up at sleepovers by asking "Would you still be my friend if . . . ," which inspired some quizzes in this book.) I also want to thank my dear friends Julie Holop, Jordann Nunn, Danielle Panabaker, and Krissy Shaffer, who continue to bring me encouragement and happiness.

This book (and my life) wouldn't be possible without my four wonderful parents: Manny and Tania Francisco, and Dan and Wendy Burton. Thank you for making me the woman I am today.

Finally, thank you to my biggest source of support and inspiration, my husband Greg St. Clair. I love you with all my heart.

Introduction

No matter if you've known your best friend since preschool or just recently became besties, you're likely always learning new things about each other. Things like:

- Your ultimate celebrity crush
- What you both *really* want to do after high school
- Your most embarrassing habits
- Your most awkward moments

But, between your epic sleepovers and long study sessions, you may not have too much time for regular heart-to-hearts or laugh-so-hard-you-cry conversations. And that's where this book comes in: to encourage you and your BFF to find some time among homework, activities, and all of your obligations to really bond—and most of all, have fun.

You and your bestie are already super close. From hearing about your most embarrassing crushes and witnessing your biggest accomplishments to cheering you up when you're sad, you and your BFF have been there for each other in good times and in bad. No book could create that!

However, no matter how tight you are, it never hurts to get a little closer. Sharing crazy secrets and laughing hysterically over inside jokes are two ways to do just that, and so is learning some new info about your closest friend to get a better sense of who she really is inside. (And she, you!)

This book was written to help you do all of those things. With these quizzes, you'll find out fun facts like each other's craziest childhood habits, and which fictional characters you'd each totally be BFFs with in real life. These quizzes also give you the chance to talk about what you each look for in a friend, and your futures when you discuss your ultimate life goals.

How to Use This Book

There's no right or wrong way to use this book, as long as you have fun! You may decide to do all the quizzes with just one friend, or—if you have more than one bestie—you may want to invite all of your BFFs over to share in the fun. You could bust it out at sleepovers, at lunch, or during downtime after school. You could read it cover to cover, or totally skip around. There are no rules!

Also, just FYI: because this book is written for all types of best friends, some questions may not apply to you and your number one pal (like, if your best friend is a guy or goes to a different school than you do). But rather than skip over those questions, be creative and figure out how you *can* make them work for you. It's your book, so do what you want!

About the Quizzes

All of the quizzes in this book are designed to help you talk about your lives, laugh a lot, and think back on your best times with your BFF. Here are the different types you'll find:

TRUTH: Interview each other to find out how you really feel about life, love, guys, your parents, and a bunch of other topics.

DO YOU DARE?: You can't have truth without dare, right?! Maybe grab a bunch of your pals and see who's willing to do what—then write down who took the dare, and when! (Clearly, you shouldn't pressure a friend into doing something she doesn't want to. Be cool, okay?)

THIS OR THAT: Choose your answers from a series of "either/or" questions to see how you and your bestie match up. Circle your choice!

THINK FAST: Try to answer these questions as quickly as you can—without thinking too much about them. (Or better yet, see if you can accurately answer for each other.)

WHAT WOULD YOU DO?: Faced with these potential (and hypothetical) situations, you two will determine how you'd react, sparking some interesting conversations.

CHECKLIST: Using these lists, you and your BFF can check off each of your preferences, allowing you to compare how you're similar—and different.

WOULD YOU STILL HANG OUT WITH ME IF . . . : Inspired by a real-life sleepover game, these quizzes present super crazy situations in which you have to decide what it would take for you to stop being friends. Circle yes, no, or maybe depending on your answer.

Final Word

Okay, besties, it's go time. Grab your BFF(s) and let the quizzing begin!

1. This or That:

HOW WOULD YOU DESCRIBE YOURSELF? (PART 1)

1. Happy-go-lucky   -or-   pessimistic?

2. More logical   -or-   more emotional?

3. Friendly   -or-   unfriendly?

4. Spontaneous   -or-   cautious?

5. Wound up   -or-   relaxed?

6. Go-getting   -or-   go-with-the-flow?

7. Gullible   -or-   skeptical?

8. Decisive   -or-   second-guessing?

9. Outgoing   -or-   shy?

10. Book-smart   -or-   street-smart?

11. Confident   -or-   self-conscious?

2. Think Fast:

TELL ME ABOUT ME

1. My best quality: _____

   _____

2. My most annoying quality: _____

   _____

3. My best talent: _____

   _____

4. Your favorite memory of ours: _____

   _____

   _____

5. Your favorite inside joke of ours: _____

   _____

   _____

6. My best physical feature: _____

   _____

7. The most unique thing about me: _____

   _____

8. What makes me a good friend: _____

   _____

   _____

9. What made you want to be my friend: _____

   _____

   _____

10. Your prediction for my future: _____

    _____

    _____

11. Your prediction for our friendship: _____

    _____

    _____

3. Truth:
WHO SHOULD WE BE?

1. What is your dream job?

_____

_____

2. Who is your role model?

_____

_____

3. If you could ask your role model any question, what would it be?

_____

_____

4. If you could be any celebrity for a day, who would it be?

_____

_____

5. As that celebrity, what would you do?

_____

_____

6. If you could do anything after high school, what would you do?

_____

_____

7. What do you think you'll be like when you're 30?

_____

_____

8. What are your top three goals for the future?

_____

_____

9. How do you think you'll try to accomplish these goals?

_____

_____

10. Do you think you'll get married and/or have kids someday?

_____

_____

4. Checklist:
DO YOU POSSESS ANY OF THESE TALENTS? (PART 1)

- ○ Juggle
- ○ Unicycle
- ○ Run a six-minute mile
- ○ Write with your feet
- ○ Type crazy fast

- ○ Perform a magic trick
- ○ Tap dance
- ○ Burp on command
- ○ Tie a cherry stem with your tongue
- ○ Do the high jump

5. This or That:
WHO WOULD YOU RATHER HANG WITH . . .

1. The President   -or-   The First Lady?

2. Tavi Gevinson   -or-   Malala Yousafzai?

3. Taylor Lautner   -or-   Rob Pattinson?

4. Kevin Durant   -or-   LeBron James?

5. Maria Sharapova   -or-   Lisa Leslie?

6. Beyoncé   -or-   Adele?

7. Tina Fey   -or-   Mindy Kaling?

8. Emma Stone   -or-   Zooey Deschanel?

9. Selena Gomez   -or-   Demi Lovato?

10. The Jonas Brothers   -or-   One Direction?

11. Miley Cyrus   -or-   Taylor Swift?

12. Zac Efron   -or-   Channing Tatum?

6. Truth:
BEING A TEENAGER

1. What's the best part about being a teenager?

_____

_____

2. What's the most annoying thing about being a teenager?

_____

_____

3. What's the number one thing you're looking forward to about being older?

_____

_____

4. What will you miss about being the age you are now when you're in your 20s?

_____

_____

5. If you could give your younger self some advice, what would you say?

_____

_____

6. If you could give your older self a message from the past, what would it be?

_____

_____

7. What's the ideal age to be, in your opinion?

_____

_____

8. If you had a younger sister, what advice would you give her about being a teenager?

_____

_____

9. What one word sums up being a teenager?

_____

_____

7. Would You Still Hang Out with Me If...

(PART 1)

1. I were nine feet tall?

       Yes   No   Maybe

2. I breathed fire?

       Yes   No   Maybe

3. I had a mermaid tail?

       Yes   No   Maybe

4. I had six arms?

       Yes   No   Maybe

5. I had skin like a snail?

       Yes   No   Maybe

6. I had snakes for hair?

       Yes   No   Maybe

7. My face suddenly turned lime green?

       Yes   No   Maybe

8. I had a lizard tongue?

       Yes   No   Maybe

9. I had a unicorn horn on my forehead?

       Yes   No   Maybe

10. I grew fur on my hands?

       Yes   No   Maybe

8. What Would You Do?
(TOTALLY HYPOTHETICAL SITUATIONS PART 1)

1. If you could live in any time period, which would you choose?

2. If you could go back to one day in history, which day would it be?

3. If you could live as anyone else for a day, who would it be?

4. If you could go back to one day in the past and change something, what would you change?

_____

5. If you could visit one point in the future, how far ahead would you go?

_____

6. If you could go back in time to apologize to someone, who would it be?

_____

7. If you had to live one day over and over and over again, forever, which would it be?

_____

8. What age or year would you least like to go back to?

_____

9. If you had to become an animal or other nonhuman living thing for the rest of your life, what would it be?

_____

10. If you could stay one age forever, what would it be?

_____

9. Think Fast:

AGREE OR DISAGREE WITH THESE SAYINGS?

1. The best things in life are free.

   Agree   Disagree

2. Keep your friends close and your enemies closer.

   Agree   Disagree

3. There's no place like home.

   Agree   Disagree

4. You can do anything you set your mind to.

   Agree   Disagree

5. If you want something done right, do it yourself.

   Agree   Disagree

6. You can't always get what you want.

   Agree   Disagree

7. Actions speak louder than words.

   Agree   Disagree

8. You can't judge a book by its cover.

       Agree   Disagree

9. If you don't have anything nice to say, don't say anything at all.

       Agree   Disagree

10. Slow and steady wins the race.

       Agree   -   Disagree

10. Checklist:
YOUR DREAM PROM DRESS

○ Lots of tulle

○ Fun, bright color

○ Glamorous

○ Goes to the floor

○ Trendy

○ Halter

○ Short and sassy

○ Comfortable

○ Sophisticated

○ Metallic color

○ Girly

○ Sparkly

○ Classic

○ Strapless

○ Black

11. This or That:

SUMMER VACATION GOALS

1.   Day camp   -or-   sleepaway camp?

2.   Sleep in   -or-   rise early?

3.   Camping   -or-   sightseeing?

4.   Get a job   -or-   laze around?

5.   Go to the beach   -or-   hang at the pool?

6.   Make ice pops   -or-   make lemonade?

7.   See a movie   -or-   at the drive-in?
     in the park

8.   Visit a farm   -or-   visit a planetarium?

9.   Do volunteer work -or-   help out your family?

10. Visit a water park -or- an amusement park?

12. Truth:

YOUR MOST EMBARRASSING MOMENTS

1. What's the most embarrassing TV show you watch?

_____

_____

2. Which movie are you most embarrassed about liking?

_____

_____

3. What's the most embarrassing song you've ever made up?

_____

_____

4. Who is your most embarrassing crush?

_____

_____

5. What's your most embarrassing habit?

_____

_____

6. What was your most embarrassing moment ever?

_____

_____

7. When have you accidentally embarrassed someone
else?

_____

_____

8. What's the most embarrassing thing in your bedroom?

_____

_____

9. What's the most embarrassing thing your parents have
ever said?

_____

_____

10. Who embarrasses you more, your mom or your dad?

_____

_____

13. Do You Dare?
(PART 1)

1. "Like" your crush's latest Facebook post, no matter what it is

   _____

2. Put a pair of underwear on your head and do a silly dance for 20 seconds

   _____

3. Take and post a selfie right now, no prepping or primping

   _____

4. Go to the bathroom, turn out the lights, and say "Bloody Mary" three times into the mirror

   _____

5. Close your eyes and act out that you're kissing your crush

   _____

6. Pretend to be an animal until everyone else guesses which one it is

   _____

7. Smell someone else's bare foot

_____

8. Create a one-minute YouTube video of yourself singing a song

_____

9. Kiss a stuffed animal for 15 seconds

_____

10. Let the group give you an extreme "makeover" with all of their makeup

_____

14. Checklist:

DO YOU POSSESS ANY OF THESE TALENTS? (PART 2)

- Baton twirling
- Matchmaking
- Ventriloquism
- Double-Dutch jump roping
- Yodeling
- Beatboxing
- Card shuffling
- Breakdancing
- Talking in an accent
- Gleeking

15. This or That:
ACTIVITIES YOU LOVE MOST

1.   Ice skating   -or-   roller skating?

2.   Jazz   -or-   ballet?

3.   Movies   -or-   plays?

4.   Soccer   -or-   softball?

5.   Fishing   -or-   hiking?

6.   Tap dancing   -or-   modern dance?

7.   Skateboarding   -or-   rollerblading?

8.   Riding bikes   -or-   riding scooters?

9.   Shopping   -or-   scavenger hunting?

10. Doing makeovers   -or-   doing crafts?

11. Singing in the chorus -or- playing a sport?

16. Checklist:
YOUR DREAM JOB

- Actress/singer
- Helping other people
- Scientist
- Nurse
- Working with animals
- Teacher
- Working in a museum
- Astronaut

- Working in nature
- Engineer
- Working with your hands
- Farmer
- Making lots of money
- Doctor
- Working toward a greater good

17. What Would You Do?
(OMG SITUATIONS)

1. If you saw a shark while swimming in the ocean?

_____

_____

_____

2. If you had to throw up in the middle of class?

_____

_____

_____

3. If you wet your pants while on a date?

_____

_____

_____

4. If you saw someone choking in a restaurant?

_____

_____

_____

5. If your best friend called you from jail?

_____

_____

_____

6. If your house was on fire?

_____

_____

_____

7. If you somehow got arrested?

_____

_____

_____

8. If your whole body broke out in bright red hives during school?

_____

_____

_____

9. If you broke your leg the week before prom?

_____

_____

_____

18. Truth:
YOUR FAMILY

1. Where's your favorite place to go with your family?

   _____

   _____

2. What's the best family vacation you've ever gone on?

   _____

   _____

3. What's the worst family vacation you've ever gone on?

   _____

   _____

4. Who's your favorite family member?

   _____

   _____

5. Who's your least favorite family member?

   _____

   _____

6. Who's your funniest family member?

_____

_____

7. What's your happiest memory of growing up?

_____

_____

8. What's your favorite game to play with your family?

_____

_____

9. What's your favorite place to eat with your family?

_____

_____

10. What's your favorite meal your parents make?

_____

_____

19. This or That:
YOUR DREAM GUY

1.   Blue   -or-   brown eyes?

2.   Curly   -or-   straight hair?

3.   Long   -or-   short hair?

4.   Light   -or-   dark hair?

5.   Buff   -or-   slim?

6.   Tall   -or-   average height?

7.   Scruffy   -or-   clean-shaven?

20. Would You Still Hang Out with Me If . . .
(PART 2)

1. I started a rumor about you?

      Yes   No   Maybe

2. I kissed your boyfriend?

      Yes   No   Maybe

3. I had no other friends at school?

       Yes   No   Maybe

4. I became a bully?

       Yes   No   Maybe

5. I started dressing like a boy?

       Yes   No   Maybe

6. Your crush started liking me instead?

       Yes   No   Maybe

7. I got a tattoo?

       Yes   No   Maybe

8. I got a piercing on my cheek?

       Yes   No   Maybe

9. I dropped out of school?

       Yes   No   Maybe

21. Think Fast:
WHAT WOULD YOU NAME . . . ?

1. Your pet dog: _____

2. Your pet cat: _____

3. Your pet hamster: _____

4. Your pet turtle: _____

5. Your future boy child: _____

6. Your future girl child: _____

7. Your pet horse: _____

8. Your pet bunny: _____

9. Your pet tarantula: _____

10. Your imaginary boyfriend: _____

11. Your fairy godmother: _____

22. Truth:
YOUR PARENTS

1. How close are you with your parents?

_____

_____

_____

2. Do you have different relationships with your mom and with your dad?

_____

_____

_____

3. What do you think your parents do best, as far as parenting goes?

_____

_____

_____

4. What are they not so good at?

_____

_____

_____

5. Are there certain things you think your parents just don't understand about you?

_____

_____

_____

6. What's the worst thing you've ever been grounded for?

_____

_____

_____

7. What are you most grateful to your parents for?

_____

_____

_____

8. Do you feel loved by your parents?

_____

_____

_____

9. Do you ever feel like you don't appreciate your parents enough?

_____

_____

_____

10. What have your parents taught you about being an adult?

_____

_____

_____

11. What have your parents taught you about marriage?

_____

_____

_____

12. What have your parents taught you about parenting?

_____

_____

_____

23. Checklist:
PLACES TO GO ON YOUR BUCKET LIST

- ○ Paris
- ○ South Africa
- ○ England
- ○ Greece
- ○ Italy
- ○ China
- ○ Brazil
- ○ Thailand

- ○ Switzerland
- ○ Tahiti
- ○ Ireland
- ○ Russia
- ○ Egypt
- ○ Japan
- ○ Costa Rica

24. Do You Dare?
(PART 2)

1. Let the group play "Light as a Feather, Stiff as a Board" with you

   _____

2. Put five crackers in your mouth and try to whistle

   _____

3. Pick someone and do the tango with her for 30 seconds

_____

4. Eat a piece of dog kibble

_____

5. Stand on the street corner with a sign that says "free hugs"

_____

6. Give the group your best Taylor Swift impression

_____

7. Go to your crush's Instagram and "like" one of his photos from at least a month ago

_____

8. Pretend to be one of your teachers until the group guesses who it is

_____

9. Let the group wrap you from head to toe in toilet paper (leaving a hole for your mouth so you can breathe!)

_____

10. Put "I'm awesome" as your Facebook status until someone else likes it

---

25. This or That:
GETTING ZEN AND PAMPERED

1. Manicure -or- pedicure?

2. Foot massage -or- scalp massage?

3. Hot stone massage -or- deep tissue massage?

4. Body wrap -or- body scrub?

5. Getting a facial -or- getting your makeup done professionally?

6. Sauna -or- steam room?

7. Jacuzzi -or- pool?

8. Acupuncture -or- aromatherapy?

9. Yoga -or- Pilates?

10. Meditation -or- journaling?

26. Think Fast:

WHEN YOU WERE A KID

1. First word you said: _____

2. Favorite toy: _____

3. Favorite stuffed animal: _____

4. Thing you were most scared of: _____

_____

5. Favorite game: _____

6. Favorite place in your house: _____

_____

7. Favorite place to hide: _____

8. Weirdest habit: _____

9. Favorite thing to wear: _____

10. Favorite friend: _____

11. Favorite make-believe place or person: _____

_____

12. Favorite food: _____

27. What Would You Do?

(TOTALLY HYPOTHETICAL SITUATIONS PART 2)

1. If you found out you're really a princess?

_____

_____

_____

2. If you had one day to do anything you wanted, no consequences?

_____

_____

_____

3. If your parents told you that you had to move across the country?

_____

_____

_____

4. If your parents told you that you had to move to *another* country?

_____

_____

_____

5. If you won the lottery?

_____

_____

_____

6. If a YouTube video you made went viral?

_____

_____

_____

7. If you answered a knock at your front door and it was the president?

_____

_____

_____

8. If you were asked to dance or sing at Lincoln Center in New York City?

_____

_____

_____

9. If you found out that your parents weren't your biological parents?

_____

_____

_____

10. If you found out that one of your siblings was really adopted?

_____

_____

_____

28. Truth:

YOUR SIBLINGS

1. How close are you to your siblings?

   _____

   _____

   _____

2. What do you love most about your relationships with
   them?

   _____

   _____

   _____

3. What's the best thing about having a sibling?

   _____

   _____

   _____

4. What are your biggest pet peeves about your siblings?

_____

_____

_____

5. What fights do you have over and over again with your siblings?

_____

_____

_____

6. How do you think having siblings has made growing up better?

_____

_____

_____

7. How has it made growing up more difficult?

_____

_____

_____

8. Do you think your parents ever play favorites?

_____

_____

_____

9. If you're an only child, have you ever wanted siblings?

_____

_____

_____

10. If you have siblings, have you ever wished you were an only child?

_____

_____

_____

29. Would You Still Hang Out with Me If...

(PART 3)

1. I decided to stop showering?

    Yes   No   Maybe

2. I decided to start wearing diapers again?

    Yes   No   Maybe

3. I started wearing a large paper bag instead of clothing?

    Yes   No   Maybe

4. I wore petrified roly polys as earrings?

    Yes   No   Maybe

5. I never brushed my teeth ever again?

    Yes   No   Maybe

6. I got Botox?

    Yes   No   Maybe

7. I shaved my eyebrows off?

    Yes   No   Maybe

8. I cut my hair into a (non-ironic) mullet?

    Yes   No   Maybe

9. I painted red circles on my cheeks as permanent "blush"?

    Yes   No   Maybe

30. This or That:
CRAZY PLACES (REAL AND FAKE) YOU'D RATHER GO

1.	To the moon	-or-	to Mars?
2.	Middle-earth	-or-	Narnia?
3.	To the center of the earth	-or-	the bottom of the ocean?
4.	Wonderland	-or-	Fantasia?
5.	To the sun	-or-	to the Milky Way?
6.	Panem	-or-	Hogwarts?
7.	Inside the human body	-or-	inside an animal?
8.	Never-Never Land	-or-	Oz?

| 9. | Bikini Bottom | -or- | Candy Land? |
| 10. | Whoville | -or- | Halloweentown? |

31. Checklist:
YOUR IDEAL GIRLS' NIGHT OUT

○ Going to the mall

○ Dancing at a party

○ Meeting up with guys

○ Listening to good music

○ Having dinner at our fave restaurant

○ Going out for frozen yogurt

○ Making new inside jokes

○ Getting dressed up

○ Pretending we're older than we are

○ Laughing hysterically over nothing

○ Trying out new makeup and hair styles

○ Doing something creative

○ Staying in and vegging

32. Truth:
YOUR FAVORITE HOLIDAYS

1. What's your absolute favorite holiday and why?

_____

_____

_____

2. What's your least favorite holiday?

_____

_____

_____

3. What rituals does your family have surrounding the holidays?

_____

_____

_____

4. Which are your favorite rituals? Least favorite?

_____

_____

_____

5. Is there anything about the holidays that you hate or find annoying?

_____

_____

_____

6. When you're an adult, what will you change about how you celebrate the holidays?

_____

_____

_____

7. What rituals or celebrations will you want to pass on to your own kids?

_____

_____

_____

8. What are your favorite holiday foods?

_____

_____

_____

9. How do you think celebrating the holidays changes as you grow up?

_____

_____

_____

10. What's the best holiday gift you've ever given someone?

_____

_____

_____

11. What's the best holiday gift you've received? Who gave it to you?

_____

_____

_____

33. Think Fast:
AT SCHOOL

1. Favorite teacher: _____

2. Least favorite teacher: _____

3. Cutest teacher: _____

4. Favorite year of school so far: _____

5. Best class: _____

6. Worst class: _____

7. Best field trip: _____

8. Worst field trip: _____

9. Best dress-up day: _____

10. Favorite school tradition: _____

11. Best coach: _____

12. Worst coach: _____

13. Favorite afterschool activity: _____

_____

14. Favorite hot lunch item: _____

15. Best place to eat lunch: _____

34. This or That:
WHAT GROSS THING WOULD YOU RATHER DO (IN THEORY)?

1.   Eat a jar of ketchup   -or-   mustard?

2.   Wear the same   -or-   the same socks
           underwear   for a year?

3.	Drink a glass of vegetable oil	-or-	white vinegar?
4.	Lick a toilet seat	-or-	a bathroom door handle?
5.	Kiss the grossest guy in school on the cheek	-or-	have him kiss you on the cheek?
6.	Put on a wet bathing suit	-or-	wear a frozen bra?
7.	Get gum in your hair	-or-	have a bird poop on you?
8.	Swallow a live slug	-or-	a live goldfish?
9.	Smell throw up	-or-	an unflushed toilet for an hour?
10.	Pet a giant centipede	-or-	a giant spider?

35. Truth:

HAVE YOU EVER . . .

1. Skipped school?

2. Pretended to be sick?

_____

3. Cheated on a test?

_____

4. Gossiped about a friend?

_____

5. Told a lie to a friend?

_____

6. Told a lie to your parents?

_____

7. Told a lie to a teacher?

_____

8. Talked your way out of getting in trouble?

_____

9. Acted differently to impress a guy?

_____

10. Done something mean to a frenemy or someone you didn't like?

_____

36. Checklist:
FAVORITE THINGS TO DO ON A DATE

- Go to a movie
- Cook dinner together
- Have him plan a surprise for you
- Go shopping
- Have a picnic in the park
- Go to a fair or carnival
- Play music together
- Walk your dogs together
- Go to a comedy show or play
- Go to a cooking class
- Check out a concert
- Go on a double date with your BFF and her BF
- Visit a museum or art show
- Go on a hike

37. This or That:
WHAT KIND OF GUY IS MORE ATTRACTIVE?

1. Smart -or- funny?

2. Tough -or- mild-mannered?

3.	Bad boy	-or-	guy your parents would approve of?
4.	Romantic	-or-	plays hard to get?
5.	Jock	-or-	musician?
6.	Nerd	-or-	slacker?
7.	Good singer	-or-	good dancer?
8.	Loner	-or-	BMOC (big man on campus)?
9.	Mysterious	-or-	what you see is what you get?
10.	Outdoorsy nature lover	-or-	city-dwelling hipster?

38. Truth:
YOUR FIRSTS (PART 1)

1. What's your first memory?

_____

_____

_____

2. When, where, and with whom was your first kiss?

_____

_____

_____

3. When was the first time your heart was broken?

_____

_____

_____

4. What was the first big-time injury you incurred?

_____

_____

_____

5. When was the first time you failed at something?

_____

_____

_____

6. When was the first time you stood up to someone?

_____

_____

_____

7. When was the first time you stood up for someone else?

_____

_____

_____

8. When was your first time being away from home?

_____

_____

_____

9. When was the first time you ever went to a hospital?

_____

_____

_____

10. When was the first time you went to a wedding?

_____

_____

_____

11. When was the first time you went to a funeral?

_____

_____

_____

39. Would You Still Hang Out with Me If…
(PART 4)

1. All I posted on Instagram were awkward selfies?

   Yes   No   Maybe

2. I only spoke in Internet slang (as in, BRB and TTYL)?

   Yes   No   Maybe

3. I burped after each sentence I said?

   Yes   No   Maybe

4. I could only communicate by farting?

   Yes   No   Maybe

5. I unfriended you on Facebook during a fight?

   Yes   No   Maybe

6. I asked the nerdiest guy in our class to a dance?

   Yes   No   Maybe

7. I turned my Twitter account into a TMI play-by-play of my life?

   Yes   No   Maybe

8. I wore a homemade plastic-wrap dress to homecoming?

   Yes   No   Maybe

9. I started a campaign for myself to get voted prom queen?

   Yes   No   Maybe

10. I decided to communicate via text and social media by only using emoji?

    Yes   No   Maybe

40. Think Fast:

SAY THE FIRST THING THAT COMES TO MIND

1. The guy you'd most like to kiss: _____

   _____

2. Your closest friend: _____

   _____

3. Your worst enemy: _____

   _____

4. Your favorite place on Earth: _____

   _____

5. Your best talent: _____

6. Your biggest fear: _____

7. The best song to dance to: _____

   _____

8. The best song to pump you up: _____

   _____

9. The celebrity you'd most like to marry: _____

_____

10. Your best physical feature: _____

_____

11. What you're most self-conscious about: _____

_____

12. Outfit you look cutest in: _____

_____

41. Do You Dare?
(PART 3)

1. Eat a spoonful of spicy mustard

_____

2. Let someone "pie" you in the face with whipped cream

_____

3. Sniff everyone's shoes and report back on whose smell the best

_____

4. Let the group do your hair into a crazy style—and wear it for the rest of the day

_____

5. Facebook "poke" your crush

_____

6. Put a piece of ice in your bra until it melts

_____

7. Give the person of your choice a kiss on the cheek

_____

8. Put on your favorite rap song and bust some moves for the group

_____

9. Tell everyone a really embarrassing story about yourself

_____

10. Mimic a famous person until someone guesses who it is

_____

42. Checklist:

CRAZY FOODS YOU'D TOTALLY TRY

- Escargot (that means snails!)
- Brain
- Oysters
- Tongue
- Eyeballs
- Dried lizards
- Octopus
- Frog legs
- Liver
- Fried spiders

43. This or That:

TREAT YOURSELF

1.   Snow Cone   -or-   Icee?

2.   Frozen yogurt   -or-   ice cream?

3.   Chocolate   -or-   vanilla?

4.   Ice cream sandwich   -or-   frozen candy bar?

5.   Hot chocolate   -or-   hot apple cider?

6.   Cherry   -or-   strawberry?

7.   Popcorn   -or-   nachos?

8.	Salsa	-or-	guacamole?
9.	Popsicle	-or-	sorbet?
10.	S'more	-or-	just-baked chocolate chip cookie?

44. Truth:
MORE OF YOUR FIRSTS (PART 2)

1. What was the first concert you ever went to?

_____

_____

2. What was the first vacation you took?

_____

_____

3. What was the first state you went to outside of your own?

_____

_____

4. What was the first country you've been to outside of the U.S.?

_____

_____

5. What was your first pet?

_____

_____

6. What was the first book you remember reading?

_____

_____

7. What was your first major accomplishment?

_____

_____

8. What was your first major disappointment?

_____

_____

9. Who was your first celebrity crush?

_____

_____

10. When was your first sleepover?

_____

_____

11. When was the first time you felt unsure of yourself?

_____

_____

45. Checklist:
YOUR LIFE GOALS

○ Go to college

○ Study abroad in college

○ Get married

○ Never have to work

○ Live in a foreign country

○ Have kids

○ Retire early

○ Go to graduate school

○ Become rich

○ Become an expert at something

○ Become famous

o Become someone's role model

o Earn enough money to give to charity

o Get a job you love

46. Think Fast:

YOUR POP CULTURE BESTIES

1. Fictional TV character you most identify with: _____

_____

2. Fictional book character you most identify with: _____

_____

3. Celebrity you think you would be BFFs with IRL: _____

_____

4. Your favorite Harry Potter character: _____

_____

5. Favorite Disney princess: _____

_____

6. Favorite Disney villain: _____

_____

7. Best character from *The Hunger Games*: _____

_____

8. Best character from *The Vampire Diaries*: _____

_____

9. Favorite member of One Direction: _____

_____

47. This or That:
FAVE FOODS

1.   Pizza   -or-   pasta?

2.   Taco   -or-   burrito?

3.   Chicken wings   -or-   french fries?

4.   Hot dog   -or-   hamburger?

5.   Steak   -or-   ham?

6.   Sushi   -or-   chow mein?

7.   Cereal   -or-   oatmeal?

8.   Coffee   -or-   tea?

9.	Waffles	-or-	pancakes?
10.	Ramen	-or-	Easy Mac?
11.	Pork bacon	-or-	tofu bacon?
12.	Peanut butter	-or-	deli meat sandwich?
13.	Green salad	-or-	fruit salad?

48. Truth:
YOUR LOVE LIFE

1. How many significant relationships have you had?

_____

_____

_____

2. Do you prefer serious relationships or flings?

_____

_____

_____

3. What's the craziest thing you ever did for love?

_____

_____

_____

4. What's your go-to flirting technique?

_____

_____

_____

5. What is love, in your opinion?

_____

_____

_____

6. Have you ever written someone a love letter?

_____

_____

_____

7. Have you ever said "I love you" to someone other than family members?

_____

_____

_____

8. When's the last time you fell in love?

_____

_____

_____

9. How do you think love changes over time?

_____

_____

_____

10. What do you think it will take to want to spend your whole life with someone?

_____

_____

_____

49. Truth:

FEELING THAT TOUGH LOVE

1. Have you ever been dumped?

_____

_____

_____

2. Have you ever dumped someone?

_____

_____

_____

3. What's your biggest relationship regret?

_____

_____

_____

4. Have you ever had a crush on someone who had a crush on someone else?

_____

_____

_____

5. What's the worst thing a former crush has ever done to you?

_____

_____

_____

6. Have you ever gotten a crush on someone when you were already in a relationship?

_____

_____

_____

7. Have you ever been betrayed in a relationship?

_____

_____

_____

8. What's the most awkward thing you've ever done in a relationship?

_____

_____

_____

9. What's the hardest romantic situation you've ever been in?

_____

_____

_____

50. This or That:
YOUR BODY

1.   Attached earlobes   -or-   detached earlobes?

2.   Outie   -or-   innie belly button?

3.   Webbed toes   -or-   nonwebbed toes?

4.   Widow's peak   -or-   straight hairline?

5.   Is your second   -or-   shorter than your
          toe longer   big toe?

6.   Do you clasp your   -or-   left over right?
          hands with your right
          thumb over your left

7.   Is your right   -or-   left leg in front
                                when you sit on the
                                ground with your
                                legs crossed?

8.   Is your thumb angled   -or-   straight when you give
                                a thumbs-up sign?

9.   Small bump on   -or-   is it smooth?
          the inside of your
          upper ear

10.   Does your pinkie   -or-   to the side?
          bend straight down

51. Checklist:

FUN GOALS ON YOUR BUCKET LIST

- Swim with dolphins
- Skydive
- Take a hot air balloon ride
- Bungee jump
- Break a world record
- Learn how to ballroom dance
- Rescue a puppy
- Go whitewater rafting
- Swim with sharks
- Go on a safari
- Smash a guitar
- Smash a pie in someone's face
- Own a private beach
- Meet your favorite celebrity
- Go to the North Pole

52. Would You Still Hang Out with Me If . . .

(PART 5)

1. I drooled constantly?

    Yes   No   Maybe

2. My butt swelled to the size of two basketballs?

    Yes   No   Maybe

3. I truly believed that Justin Bieber was my real-life boyfriend?

Yes   No   Maybe

4. I had a twin growing out of my neck?

Yes   No   Maybe

5. I asked everyone to refer to me only as "The Great One"?

Yes   No   Maybe

6. I grew my hair down to my ankles?

Yes   No   Maybe

7. I stopped speaking and could only grunt to communicate?

Yes   No   Maybe

8. I started aging backward?

Yes   No   Maybe

9. I suddenly sprouted wings?

Yes   No   Maybe

10. I suddenly sprouted horns?

Yes   No   Maybe

11. I pierced a large brass bull ring through my nose?

Yes   No   Maybe

53. Think Fast:

WHICH OF OUR FRIENDS WILL . . .

1. Win an Academy Award? _____

2. Invent something really important? _____

_____

3. Win the Nobel Peace Prize? _____

_____

4. Get a job first? _____

5. Get married first? _____

6. Have a baby first? _____

7. Become an astronaut? _____

8. Become president? _____

9. Move to another country? _____

10. Climb Mount Everest? _____

11. Go totally MIA after high school? _____

_____

12. Live the longest? _____

54. Truth:
YOUR FRIENDSHIPS

1. What qualities do you look for in a friend?

_____

_____

_____

2. What do you think is the most essential part of a friendship?

_____

_____

_____

3. In what ways are friendships like romantic relationships?

_____

_____

_____

4. Would you rather have a ton of *close* friends or a few best friends?

_____

_____

_____

5. What kind of friendship do we have?

_____

_____

_____

6. Which of your friends writes the best notes and/or posts online?

_____

_____

_____

7. Which of your friends can you depend on most in case of a crisis?

_____

_____

_____

8. How have your friendships changed as you've gotten older?

_____

_____

_____

9. How have your friendships stayed the same?

_____

_____

_____

10. Are there things you want to stay the same about your friends forever?

_____

_____

_____

55. Do You Dare?
(PART 4)

1. Let your pet (or friend's pet) kiss you on the lips

_____

2. Pretend you're holding/caring for a baby for the next five minutes

_____

3. Put grapes in your nostrils, then blow them out

_____

4. Eat a Popsicle pretending that you're really making out with your crush

_____

5. Use items from the fridge to apply "makeup" on yourself

_____

6. Check your belly button and reveal if there is any lint in it

_____

7. Write a secret admirer letter to someone's younger sibling

_____

8. Smell someone's armpit

_____

9. Put hot sauce on your tongue for 30 seconds

_____

10. Knock on your neighbor's front door, then run away

_____

56. This or That:

WOULD YOU RATHER LIVE WITHOUT . . .

1.   Your cell phone   -or-   your computer?

2.   Lip gloss   -or-   mascara?

3.   Your sense of smell   -or-   your ability to hear?

4.   Your arms   -or-   your legs?

5.   Candy   -or-   soda?

6.   Your eyes   -or-   your mouth?

7.   Your hair   -or-   your fingernails?

8.   Coffee   -or-   chocolate?

9.   Spotify   -or-   your iPod?

10.   Your toothbrush   -or-   your hairbrush?

11.   The ability to ever drive   -or-   the ability to move out of your parents' house?

12.   Facebook   -or-   Instagram?

57. Checklist:
SKILLS WE WANT TO LEARN (PART 1)

- How to speak another language
- How to speak in sign language
- How to cook
- How to use power tools
- How to sew
- How to bake a cake from memory
- How to build a fire from scratch
- How to change a tire
- How to tie a guy's tie
- How to use chopsticks
- How to do CPR
- How to put on makeup like a pro

58. What Would You Do?
(YOUR FRIENDS)

1. If one of your friends had really bad body odor?

_____

_____

_____

2. If your friend had a booger on her face in the middle of a class presentation?

_____

_____

_____

3. If you knew a friend's BF liked someone else?

_____

_____

_____

4. If you knew your friend liked someone other than her BF?

_____

_____

_____

5. If you found out that your bestie told other people one of your secrets?

_____

_____

_____

6. If you found out that one of your friends' parents were getting divorced?

_____

_____

_____

7. If you overheard someone talking badly about a friend?

_____

_____

_____

8. If your BFF got a boyfriend and started becoming totally MIA?

_____

_____

_____

9. If you got a friend in trouble and she was getting all the punishment?

_____

_____

_____

10. If your bestie got grounded and couldn't go to a fun party or school dance?

_____

_____

_____

59. Truth:

WHEN'S THE LAST TIME YOU . . .

1. Laughed until you cried?

_____

_____

_____

2. Cried-cried?

_____

_____

_____

3. Felt let down by someone?

_____

_____

_____

4. Felt disappointed in yourself?

_____

_____

_____

5. Did something you regretted?

_____

_____

_____

6. Felt proud of yourself?

_____

_____

_____

7. Made someone feel awkward?

_____

_____

_____

8. Totally embarrassed yourself?

_____

_____

_____

9. Screwed up something really badly?

_____

_____

_____

10. Got so excited about something that you literally jumped for joy?

_____

_____

_____

11. Overreacted about something?

_____

_____

_____

60. This or That:

HOW WOULD YOU DESCRIBE YOURSELF? (PART 2)

1. Nature girl -or- city girl?

2. Organized -or- scatterbrained?

3. Artsy -or- science-y?

4. Beach bunny -or- snow bunny?

5. Clean freak -or- can get your hands dirty?

6. Old soul -or- act your age?

7. Naughty -or- nice?

8. Ready to grow up -or- enjoy being young?

9. Fashionable -or- create your own trends?

10. Leader -or- follower?

11. Goody-goody -or- rebel?

12. Calculating -or- easy-going?

61. Think Fast:

OUR CRUSHES THROUGH THE YEARS

1. Kindergarten: _____

2. First Grade: _____

3. Second Grade: _____

4. Third Grade: _____

5. Fourth Grade: _____

6. Fifth Grade: _____

7. Sixth Grade: _____

8. Seventh Grade: _____

9. Eighth Grade: _____

62. What Would You Do?
(YOUR—REAL OR HYPOTHETICAL—BOYFRIEND)

1. If he started talking badly about your friends?

_____

_____

_____

2. If his friends were jerks to you?

_____

_____

_____

3. If you found out he had a crush on someone else?

_____

_____

_____

4. If you found out that he wanted to give you a promise ring?

_____

_____

_____

5. If you really wanted to break up with him but didn't know how?

_____

_____

_____

6. If your parents hated him?

_____

_____

_____

7. If he suddenly had to move away to another state?

_____

_____

_____

8. If he decided to go to a different college than you?

_____

_____

_____

9. If he told his friends your deepest secrets?

_____

_____

_____

63. Truth:

WHAT DO YOU THINK ABOUT THESE DATING "RULES"?

1. The guy should always pay for the first date.

_____

_____

_____

2. If a guy texts, instead of calls, he's not that into you.

_____

_____

_____

3. You shouldn't play games when you like someone.

_____

_____

_____

4. Nobody will love you until you love yourself.

_____

_____

_____

5. If a guy teases you a lot, that means he likes you.

_____

_____

_____

6. Unless you feel fireworks, no second date.

_____

_____

_____

7. A guy should always make the first move.

_____

_____

_____

8. If you like a guy, don't make yourself too available—make him work for it.

_____

_____

_____

9. You should wait for the guy to ask about making it "official."

_____

_____

_____

10. If you love someone let him go—if he comes back to you, it's meant to be.

_____

_____

_____

11. Don't accept a last-minute date—he'll think you're desperate.

_____

_____

_____

64. Checklist:
MORE SKILLS WE WANT TO LEARN (PART 2)

- How to do a real pushup
- How to cook without a recipe
- How to shoot a bow and arrow
- How to French braid
- How to read a real map and compass
- How to build a website
- How to ride a unicycle
- How to start a business
- How to defend ourselves

○ How to draw

○ How to play an instrument

○ How to find the good stuff in a vintage store

65. Would You Still Hang Out with Me If . . .
(PART 6)

1. I had razor blades for fingernails?

   Yes   No   Maybe

2. I needed you to chew my food and spit it into my mouth like a baby bird?

   Yes   No   Maybe

3. I literally never stopped talking?

   Yes   No   Maybe

4. I got crazy plastic surgery to look like a Barbie doll?

   Yes   No   Maybe

5. I dyed my skin neon green?

   Yes   No   Maybe

6. My breath always smelled like rotten eggs?

    Yes   No   Maybe

7. I sang everything I said?

    Yes   No   Maybe

8. I styled my hair into a 3-foot Mohawk?

    Yes   No   Maybe

9. I ate only liver and onions?

    Yes   No   Maybe

10. I took a vow of silence and never spoke again?

    Yes   No   Maybe

66. Truth:

WHAT MAKES YOU LAUGH?

1. How would you describe your sense of humor?

_____

_____

2. What's the corniest joke you've ever heard?

_____

_____

3. What's the funniest joke you've ever heard?

_____

_____

4. Who is your favorite funny actor/actress?

_____

_____

5. Favorite funny movie or TV show?

_____

_____

6. What kinds of jokes or humor do you find totally not funny?

_____

_____

7. Who is your funniest friend?

_____

_____

8. Who is your funniest family member?

_____

_____

9. Would you marry a guy who wasn't funny?

_____

_____

10. When you need cheering up, what always makes you laugh?

_____

_____

67. This or That:

WHICH FICTIONAL HEROINE DO YOU IDENTIFY WITH MORE?

1. Hermione Granger   -or-   Katniss Everdeen?

2. The Powerpuff Girls   -or-   Sailor Moon?

3.   Black Widow   -or-   Storm?

4.   Wonder Woman   -or-   She-Ra?

5.   Anne of Green Gables   -or-   the Little Princess?

6.   Lara Croft   -or-   Princess Peach?

7.   Buffy the   -or-   Veronica Mars?
   Vampire Slayer

8.   Merida from *Brave*   -or-   Anna from *Frozen*?

9.   Princess Buttercup   -or-   Princess Leia?

10.   Nancy Drew   -or-   Ramona Quimby?

68. Checklist:
COOL SPORTS WE WANT TO TRY

- Paddleboarding
- Scuba diving
- Snow skiing
- Water skiing
- Wakeboarding
- Snowboarding
- Kayaking
- Hang-gliding
- Zorbing
- Ziplining
- Bobsledding
- Horseback riding
- Mountain biking
- Surfing

69. What Would You Do?

(DATING AND BOYS)

1. If you found out your crush's Facebook or e-mail password?

   _____

   _____

   _____

2. If you snorted your drink out of your nose while talking to your crush?

   _____

   _____

   _____

3. If you found out that your crush liked your bestie?

   _____

   _____

   _____

4. If a guy you kinda liked professed his love to you in front of everyone at lunch?

_____

_____

_____

5. If you liked a guy but found out he was too shy to ask you out?

_____

_____

_____

6. If you tripped and fell right in front of your crush?

_____

_____

_____

7. If you knew a guy was going to ask you to a dance but you didn't want to go with him?

_____

_____

_____

8. If a guy forwarded the private text you sent him to all of his friends?

_____

_____

_____

9. If a guy asked you out, then told you that his parents had to come with you on your date?

_____

_____

_____

70. Think Fast:

A FEW OF YOUR FAVORITE THINGS (PART 1)

1. Movie: _____

2. TV Show: _____

3. Music Genre: _____

4. Song: _____

5. Book: _____

6. Board Game: _____

7. Phone App: _____

8. Phone Game: _____

9. Video Game: _____

10. Candy: _____

11. Drink: _____

71. This or That:

WHAT KIND OF COLLEGE DO YOU WANT TO ATTEND?

1. Close   -or-   far from home?

2. Football school   -or-   liberal arts college?

3. Greek system   -or-   no sororities and fraternities?

4. In a big city   -or-   in a college town?

5. More study abroad options   -or-   more on-campus activities?

6. Coed   -or-   girls only?

7. Big   -or-   small student body?

8. Semester   -or-   quarter system?

9. Tough academics   -or-   more of a party school?

10. Religious   -or-   secular?

11. Diverse   -or-   designed for one type of student?

72. What Would You Do?
(SCHOOL SITUATIONS)

1. If you found a personal note someone dropped?

_____

_____

_____

2. If you witnessed someone getting bullied?

_____

_____

_____

3. If a bully started picking on you?

_____

_____

_____

4. If a new girl came and didn't have any friends?

_____

_____

_____

5. If you found money on the ground?

_____

_____

_____

6. If you had to give a class presentation on the spot?

_____

_____

_____

7. If you knew you could cheat without getting caught?

_____

_____

_____

8. If you saw two teachers on a date?

_____

_____

_____

9. If you could sneak into the teachers' lounge?

_____

_____

_____

10. If you could sneak into the principal's office?

_____

_____

_____

11. If you could sneak into the cafeteria kitchen?

_____

_____

_____

12. If you discovered that your diary or journal was missing from your locker?

_____

_____

_____

73. Truth:
ALL ABOUT YOUR BIRTHDAY

1. Do you like celebrating your birthday?

_____

_____

2. What's your ideal way to spend your birthday?

_____

_____

3. What was your best birthday?

_____

_____

4. What's the best birthday present you ever got?

_____

_____

5. What was your most memorable birthday party?

_____

_____

6. What's the craziest thing you ever asked for on your birthday?

_____

_____

7. What's your favorite type of birthday cake?

_____

_____

8. How do you feel about surprise parties?

_____

_____

9. Do you like when people sing "Happy Birthday" to you in public?

_____

_____

10. Would you rather people call you, e-mail you, or text you on your birthday?

_____

_____

11. Does your family have any special birthday traditions?

_____

_____

74. Do You Dare?
(PART 5)

1. Tweet a crazed fan message to your favorite celebrity

_____

2. Act like a bunny, complete with convincing nose wiggles, for two minutes

_____

3. Give a convincing imitation of the worst teacher at school

_____

4. Go outside and scream your crush's name

_____

5. Take off your socks and hang them on your ears for 10 minutes

_____

6. Text your crush just the color of your underwear (no context, no explanation)

_____

7. Put a spoonful of peanut butter in your mouth and sing "Happy Birthday"

_____

8. Call a pizza delivery line and flirt with the person who answers

_____

9. Eat a cracker off someone's stomach

_____

10. Wear someone else's bra for five minutes

_____

75. Think Fast:
WHAT WAS YOUR MOST AWKWARD MOMENT?

1. In class: _____

_____

_____

_____

2. On Facebook: _____

_____

_____

_____

3. At summer camp: _____

_____

_____

_____

4. On Instagram: _____

_____

_____

5. With a friend: _____

_____

_____

_____

6. With a teacher: _____

_____

_____

_____

7. While playing sports: _____

_____

_____

_____

8. In front of a guy: _____

_____

_____

_____

9. With your parents: _____

_____

_____

_____

10. With your sibling(s): _____

_____

_____

_____

11. Out in public: _____

_____

_____

_____

12. When you were alone: _____

_____

_____

_____

76. Checklist:
CAN YOU DO THIS? (PART 1)

- Touch your tongue to your nose
- Touch your tongue to your chin
- Raise one eyebrow
- Lick your elbow
- Roll your tongue like a wave

- Curl the sides of your tongue up
- Wiggle your nose
- Bend your thumb to your forearm
- Put your whole fist in your mouth
- Go cross-eyed

77. Truth:
BEING A GIRL

1. What's the hardest thing about being female?

_____

_____

_____

2. What's the most awesome thing about being female?

_____

_____

_____

3. In what ways do you think guys have it easier than girls?

_____

_____

_____

4. In what ways do girls have it easier than guys?

_____

_____

_____

5. Do you think both sexes are truly equal?

_____

_____

_____

6. If no, what do you think needs to happen to have equality?

_____

_____

_____

7. Are there any things about being a girl that scare you?

_____

_____

_____

8. Do you get nervous about getting your period?

_____

_____

_____

9. Do you think it's cool that only women can give birth?

_____

_____

_____

10. What did you learn from your mom or female family members about what it means to be a woman?

_____

_____

_____

78. What Would You Do?
(IF YOU WERE STUCK ON A DESERTED ISLAND)

1. If you could only have one makeup item with you, what would it be?

   _____

2. If you could only have one magazine to read?

   _____

3. One book?

   _____

4. One song to listen to?

   _____

5. One food to eat?

   _____

6. One other person who could be there with you?

   _____

7. One emergency item (like a flashlight, flare gun, matches)?

   _____

8. One animal to be friends with on the island?

_____

9. One attempt to catch the attention of a plane or boat going by?

_____

10. One comfort item (like a blanket or a stuffed animal)?

_____

11. One protective item (like sunscreen or a hat)?

_____

79. This or That:
FAVORITE JUNK FOOD

1.	Smarties	-or-	SweeTARTS?
2.	Milk	-or-	dark chocolate?
3.	Candy corn	-or-	Peeps?
4.	Peanut butter cups	-or-	Cadbury Eggs?
5.	Red Vines	-or-	Twizzlers?
6.	Malted milk balls	-or-	Raisinets?

7.	Plain M&M's	-or-	Peanut M&M's?
8.	Snickers	-or-	Milky Way?
9.	Rock candy	-or-	cotton candy?
10.	Jawbreakers	-or-	giant gumballs?
11.	Pop Rocks	-or-	Razzles?
12.	Nerds	-or-	Sour Patch Kids?
13.	Good & Plenty	-or-	Hot Tamales?
14.	Gummy bears	-or-	gummy worms?

80. Checklist:
CAN YOU DO THIS? (PART 2)

- Wiggle your ears
- Pat your head and rub your stomach
- Burp the alphabet
- Touch your toes without bending your knees
- Fold your tongue in half
- Stand on your head
- Touch your ear to your shoulder
- Make a water drop sound by flicking your cheek
- Make a "V" between your ring and middle fingers
- Put your foot behind your head

81. Think Fast:

YOUR FAVORITE BEAUTY PRODUCTS

1. Mascara: _____

2. Eye shadow color: _____

3. Body spray scent: _____

4. Perfume: _____

5. Lip gloss flavor: _____

6. Lipstick color: _____

7. Nail polish color: _____

8. Beauty tool: _____

9. Face wash: _____

10. Face lotion: _____

11. Acne fighter: _____

82. Truth:

HOW DO YOU REALLY FEEL ABOUT SOCIAL MEDIA?

1. What's the best thing social media has brought to our lives?

_____

_____

_____

2. How does it make our lives more awkward?

_____

_____

_____

3. How often is too often to post on Facebook, Instagram, and so on?

_____

_____

_____

4. What are your biggest social media pet peeves?

_____

_____

_____

5. Do you ever wish social media didn't exist? Why or why not?

_____

_____

_____

6. Would you ever consider deleting all of your social media accounts? Why or why not?

_____

_____

_____

7. How do you think you spend most of your time on social media?

_____

_____

_____

8. How do you think social media improves friendships?

_____

_____

_____

9. How do you think it helps romantic relationships?

_____

_____

_____

10. How long do you think you could go without posting on or looking at your social media accounts?

_____

_____

_____

83. Think Fast:

IF YOU WERE A [BLANK], WHAT WOULD YOU BE? (PART 1)

1. Type of car: _____

2. Animal: _____

3. Color: _____

4. Item of clothing: _____

5. Shape: _____

6. Shoe: _____

7. Superhero: _____

8. Season: _____

9. Flavor of ice cream: _____

10. Smell: _____

84. Truth:

SUPERSTITIONS AND THE SUPERNATURAL

1. Do you have any superstitions?

_____

_____

_____

2. Have you ever been afraid of the dark?

_____

_____

_____

3. Are there any rituals or things you do to ward off bad luck?

_____

_____

_____

4. Do you read (and maybe believe) your horoscope?

_____

_____

_____

5. Would you (or have you) ever had your palm read? Why or why not?

_____

_____

_____

6. Have you ever seen a ghost?

_____

_____

_____

7. Have you ever seen an alien?

_____

_____

_____

8. Have you ever had a weird supernatural experience you can't explain?

_____

_____

_____

9. Has anything ever caused the hairs on the back of your neck to stand up?

_____

_____

_____

10. What's the creepiest true story you've heard about something supernatural?

_____

_____

_____

85. Checklist:
WHAT KIND OF KID WERE YOU?

- Always got a time-out
- Got teased in school
- Had monsters in your closet
- Had an imaginary friend
- Ran away from home
- Never got in trouble
- Kind of a loner

- Played with dolls
- Got homesick a lot
- Played with trucks
- Played dress-up
- Slept with a stuffed animal
- Had a blankie
- Always had lots of friends

86. Think Fast:
A FEW MORE OF YOUR FAVORITE THINGS (PART 2)

1. Color: _____

2. Place in your house: _____

3. Place on Earth: _____

4. Day of the week: _____

5. Thing you own: _____

6. Outfit: _____

7. School subject: _____

8. Teacher: _____

9. Thing to do on a Friday night: _____

_____

10. Time of day: _____

11. Meal: _____

87. What Would You Do?
(WOULD YOU BE FRIENDS WITH SOMEONE WHO . . .)

1. Is the uncoolest kid in school? _____

_____

2. Is the biggest bully? _____

_____

3. Didn't have as much money as your family? _____

_____

4. Has a super rich family? _____

_____

5. Has special needs? _____

_____

6. Comes from a different cultural background than you?

_____

7. Has a different religion than you? _____

_____

88. This or That:

WHAT'S MORE ANNOYING?

1.	Chewing with your mouth open	-or-	smacking your gum?
2.	Whistling	-or-	humming?
3.	Not saying "thank you"	-or-	not holding the door open?
4.	Texting while someone else is talking	-or-	interrupting?
5.	Talking during a movie	-or-	cutting in line?
6.	Nose picking	-or-	nail biting?

7. Guys leaving the   -or-   not washing
   toilet seat up   their hands?

8. Making a duck face   -or-   saying "YOLO"
                                 all the time?

9. Wearing UGG boots   -or-   wearing trucker hats?
   in the summer

10. Loudly talking on your -or-   slow walking?
    cell phone in public

11. Littering   -or-   not cleaning up
                                  after your dog?

12. Being fake   -or-   spreading rumors?

89. Truth:
DO YOU BELIEVE IN . . .

1. Love at first sight? _____

_____

2. The power of positive thinking? _____

_____

3. Soulmates? _____

_____

4. God? _____

_____

5. Santa Claus? _____

_____

6. Miracles? _____

_____

7. Aliens? _____

_____

8. Ghosts? _____

_____

9. An afterlife? _____

_____

10. Yourself? _____

_____

90. This or That:

WHICH SUPERPOWER WOULD YOU RATHER HAVE?

1. To live forever   -or-   to be able to save anyone, anytime?

2. To be able to breathe underwater   -or-   to swim without ever getting tired?

3. To make anyone fall in love with you   -or-   to make anyone disappear?

4. To teleport yourself anywhere   -or-   to fly?

5. To shoot fire from your hands   -or-   shoot ice?

6. To jump super high   -or-   to run super fast?

7. To stop time   -or-   to speed up time?

8. To never have to sleep   -or-   never have to use the bathroom?

9. To give anyone an instant makeover   -or-   to heal anyone who's sick?

10.   To instantly grow   -or-   to instantly
          your hair   change your hair
                                                 color anytime?

91. Truth:
WEIRD THINGS ABOUT YOUR BODY

1. What do you think is your funniest-looking body part?

_____

2. Where's the weirdest place you have a freckle?

_____

3. What's the most embarrassing beauty or body product
   you use?

_____

4. Do you like to wax or shave your legs?

_____

5. What's your coolest scar, and how did you get it?

_____

6. Do you have any allergies?

_____

7. What's the craziest thing that's ever happened to your body (like a weird physical reaction)?

_____

8. Where are you most ticklish?

_____

92. Think Fast:

IF YOU WERE A [BLANK], WHAT WOULD YOU BE? (PART 2)

1. Fruit: _____

2. Hairstyle: _____

3. Kind of tree: _____

4. Nail polish color: _____

5. Famous person: _____

6. Insect: _____

7. Dessert: _____

8. Fabric: _____

9. Dance style: _____

10. Flower: _____

93. This or That:
WHAT'S WORSE?

1. Failing a test   -or-   getting caught cheating?

2. Falling from a big height   -or-   drowning?

3. Letting down your parents   -or-   letting down your friends?

4. Balancing at the top of a tall building   -or-   being super far underground?

5. Being a bully   -or-   getting made fun of?

6. Not getting into college   -or-   not getting a job?

7. Flunking out of school -or- losing all of your friends?

8. Starving to death -or- dying of a broken heart?

94. Truth:

WHAT'S YOUR FUNNIEST MEMORY . . . ?

1. From elementary school? _____

_____

_____

2. From when you were a baby? _____

_____

_____

3. With your parents? _____

_____

_____

4. From a family vacation? _____

_____

_____

5. With your best friend? _____

_____

_____

6. From your parents' childhood stories? _____

_____

_____

7. With one of your grandparents? _____

_____

_____

8. With your sibling(s)? _____

_____

_____

9. About one of your pets? _____

_____

_____

10. From camp or playing sports? _____

_____

_____

95. Do You Dare?
(PART 6)

1. Eat a spoonful of flour

_____

2. Drink a soda and burp your full name

_____

3. Do a cartwheel in your underwear

_____

4. Stick your hand in the toilet bowl

_____

5. Slow dance with a broom for two minutes

_____

6. Go outside and sing the national anthem full volume

_____

7. Send your crush a text using only emoji

_____

8. Knock on your neighbor's door and ask for a roll of toilet paper

_____

9. Pick your nose for 15 seconds

_____

96. Truth:
FRIENDSHIPS LOST

1. What's the biggest fight or falling out you've ever had with a friend?

_____

_____

_____

2. What's your relationship with this person like now?

_____

_____

_____

3. How would you feel if you bumped into this person randomly?

_____

_____

_____

4. Is there someone from your past you wish you still kept in touch with?

_____

_____

_____

5. What's the worst thing a friend has ever done to you?

_____

_____

_____

6. Do you have any true enemies?

_____

_____

_____

7. Have you ever had to "break up" with a friend and completely end the relationship?

_____

_____

_____

8. Have you ever betrayed a friend's trust?

_____

_____

_____

9. What's the biggest regret you have in terms of your friendships?

_____

_____

_____

10. Which friend from your past do you think had the worst influence on you?

_____

_____

_____

97. Think Fast:

WHICH OF OUR FRIENDS IS . . .

1. The most trustworthy? _____

2. The least trustworthy? _____

3. The biggest gossip? _____

4. The best secret-keeper? _____

5. The smartest? _____

6. The most popular? _____

7. The most likely to get in trouble? _____

   _____

8. The one who gets away with anything? _____

   _____

9. The prettiest? _____

10. The nicest? _____

11. The chillest? _____

98. This or That:

WHAT SCARES YOU MORE ABOUT THE FUTURE?

1. Being the last of your friends to get your period -or- being the last one to need a bra?

2. Never finding a boyfriend -or- never figuring out a career path?

3. Turning into your mom -or- turning into your dad?

4. Growing up too fast -or- never feeling grown-up enough?

5. Getting held back in high school -or- not getting into college?

6. Failing college -or- not graduating?

7. Hating your job -or- hating your boss?

8. Worrying about money -or- worrying about working too much?

9. Getting old mentally -or- physically?

10. Losing touch with friends -or- growing apart from siblings?

99. Truth:

DREAMING BIG

1. If you were to write a book, what would it be about?

_____

_____

_____

2. If you were to make a movie, what genre would it be?

_____

_____

_____

3. If you could start a charity, what would it be for?

_____

_____

_____

4. If you were to create a TV show, what kind of show would it be?

_____

_____

_____

5. If you were going to open a restaurant, what would the menu be like?

_____

_____

_____

6. If you were going to invent something revolutionary, how would it change the world?

_____

_____

_____

7. If you could open a theme park, what rides and fun stuff would it have?

8. If you were to invent a new soda or snack food, what would it be?

9. If you were a rock star, what would your band or stage name be?

10. If you were a sports icon, how would you pose on the Wheaties box?

_____

_____ _____

_____

100. Think Fast:
EVEN MORE OF YOUR FAVORITE THINGS (PART 3)

1. Sport to watch: _____

2. Sport to play: _____

3. Athlete: _____

4. Museum or landmark: _____

5. National park: _____

6. Theme park: _____

7. Restaurant: _____

8. Social media platform: _____

9. Website: _____

10. Vacation destination: _____

101. Truth:

YOU FINISHED THE BOOK QUIZ!

1. What's the most surprising thing you shared with me?

_____

_____

_____

2. What's the most surprising thing I shared with you?

_____

_____

_____

3. Were there any questions you didn't want to answer or wanted to skip?

_____

_____

_____

4. What's the most important thing you learned about me that you didn't know before?

_____

_____

_____

5. What do you think you learned about yourself?

_____

_____

_____

6. How have we become closer after learning new things about each other?

_____

_____

_____

7. Has your opinion of me changed at all after listening to my answers?

_____

_____

_____

8. Do you have any worries that my opinion of you may have changed?

_____

_____

_____

9. How did these quizzes help you appreciate our BFF-ness more?

_____

_____

_____

10. Anything else you want to ask me? (Last chance!)

_____

_____

_____

About the Author

Natasha Burton is a journalist and relationships expert whose work has appeared in *Cosmopolitan for Latinas*, *Maxim*, Cosmopolitan.com, MSN.com, WomansDay.com, DailyWorth.com, LearnVest.com, and Mom.me, among other print and online outlets.

She's the author of *101 Quizzes for Couples* (Adams Media, 2013), and the coauthor of *The Little Black Book of Big Red Flags* (Adams Media, 2011), a critically acclaimed dating guide that has been translated into multiple languages.

Burton holds a master's degree in creative writing from the University of Southern California, where she formerly taught composition. She lives in Santa Barbara, California, with her husband, Greg, and their toy Austrian Shepherd, Peyton.